Copyright © 2021 by Iman N. Drummond

All rights reserved. No part of this book may be reproduced or copied in any manner without written permission from the author. For more information, contact:
carterswaythebook@gmail.com
www.carterswaythebook.com

ISBN 978-0-578-88305-2 (paperback)

# CARTER'S WAY
## All the Things You Can Be

**IMAN DRUMMOND**

To my nephew Carter, who brings the sunshine to every room,
and has shown me a new way to love.


To all the young dreamers who can be anything they want to be.

There was a little boy named Carter, who would often dream about being a grown up. One day Carter decided to ask his Dad,...

# A
**is for Artist**

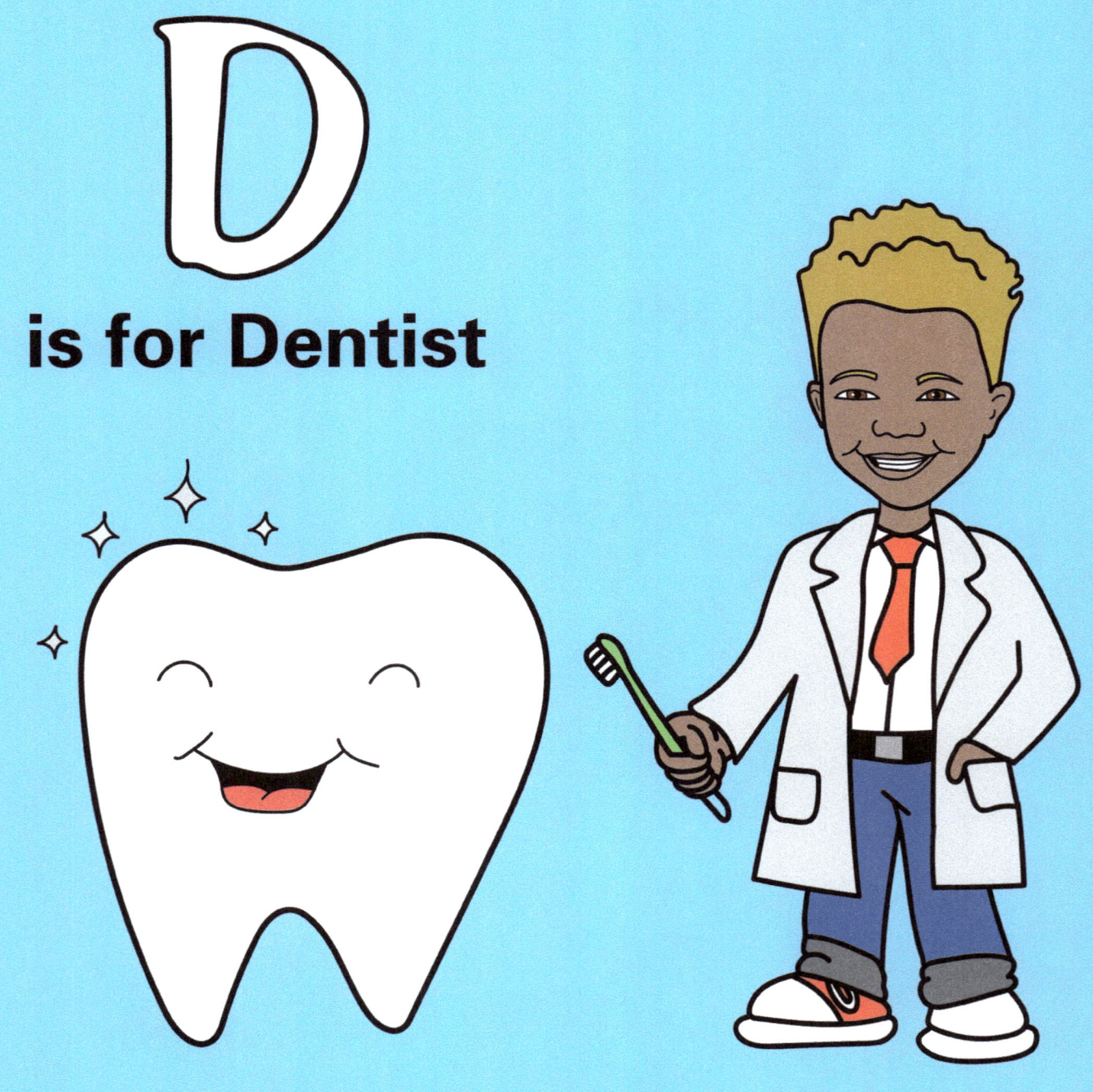

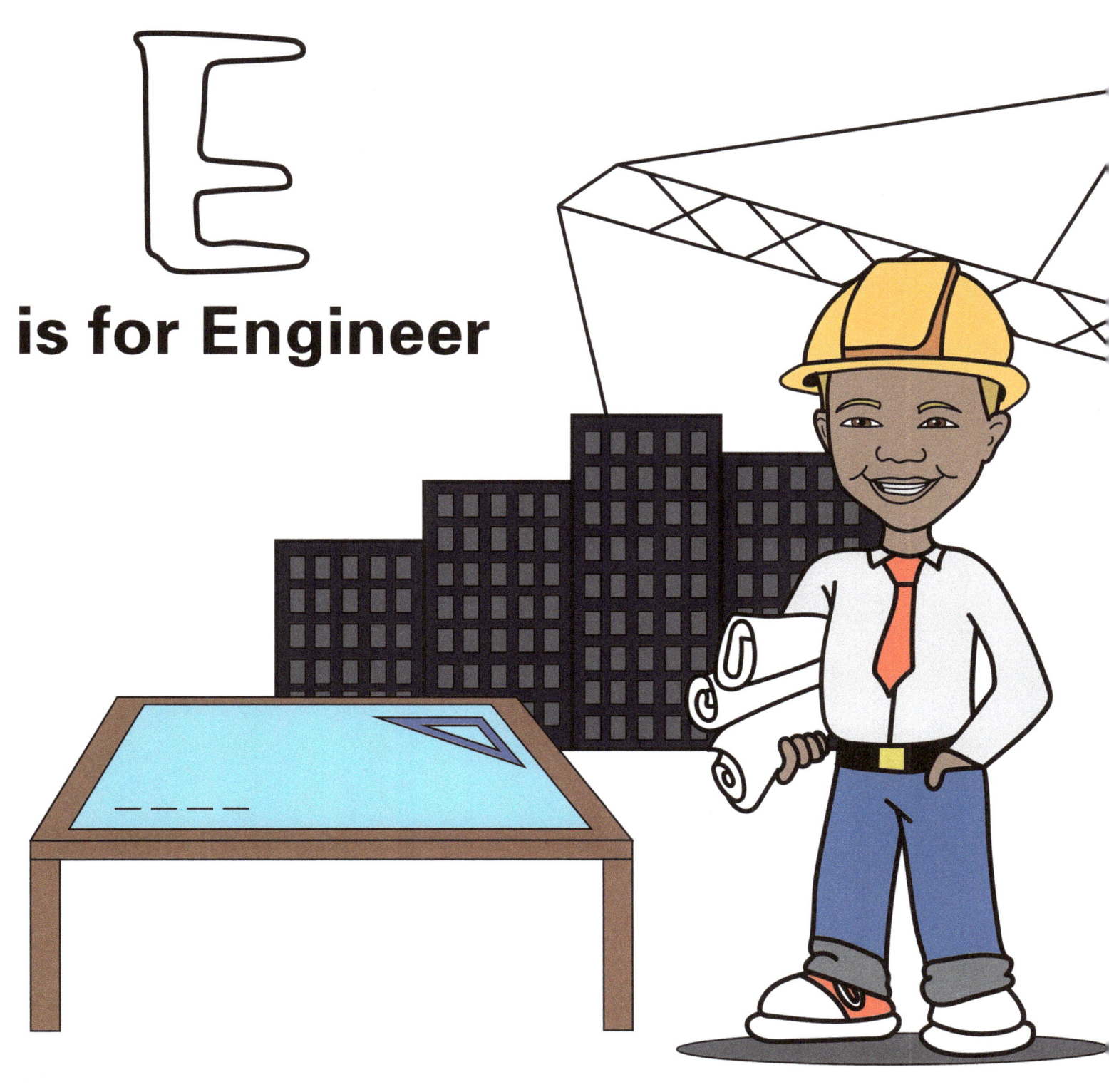

# G is for Gardener

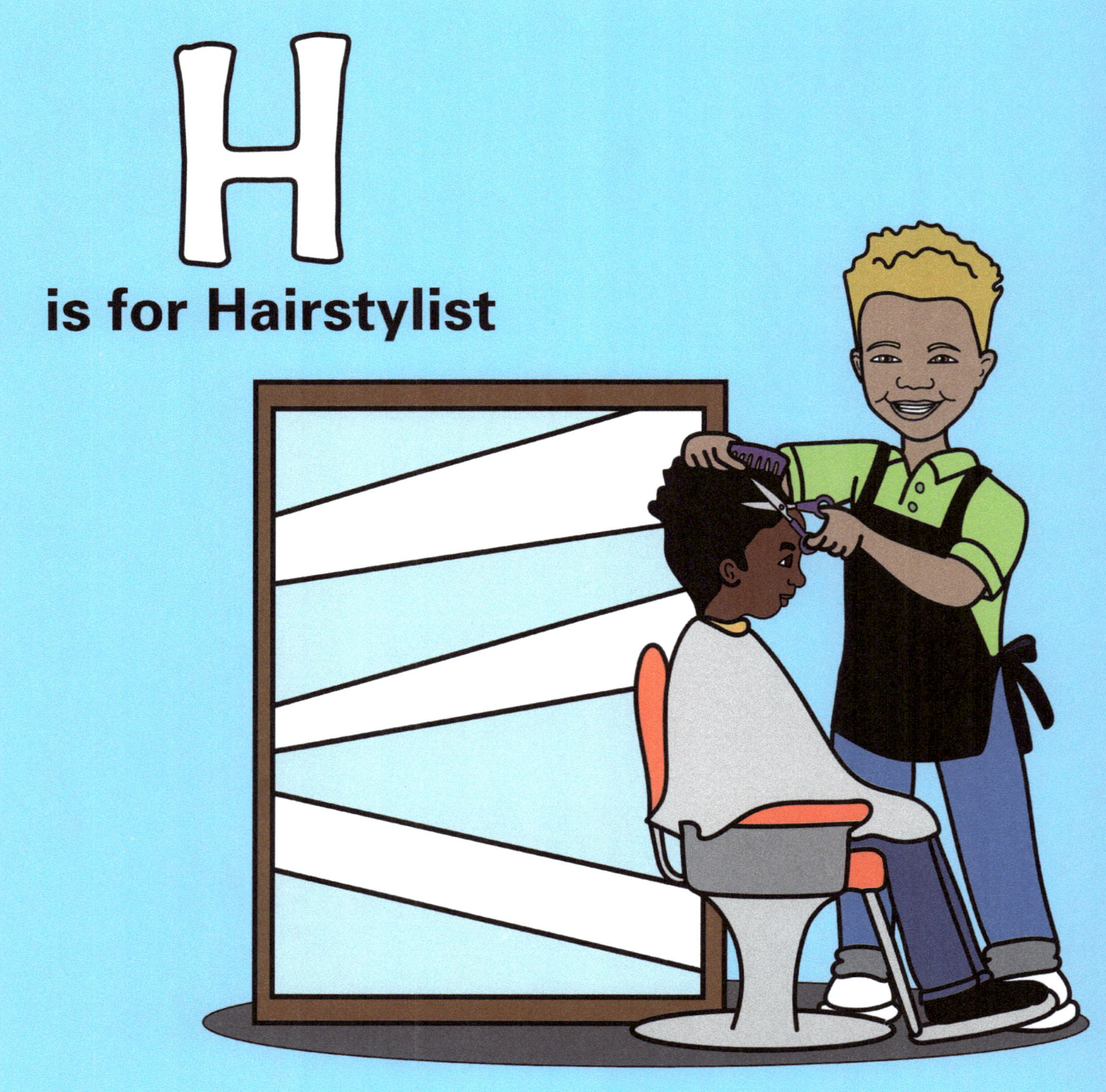

# I

is for Icecream Man

# L

is for Librarian

# O

## is for Optometrist

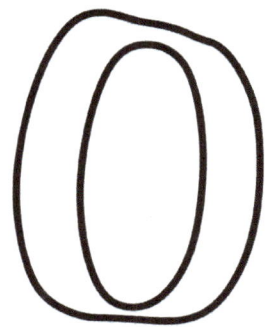

# P
**is for Pilot**

# T is for Teacher

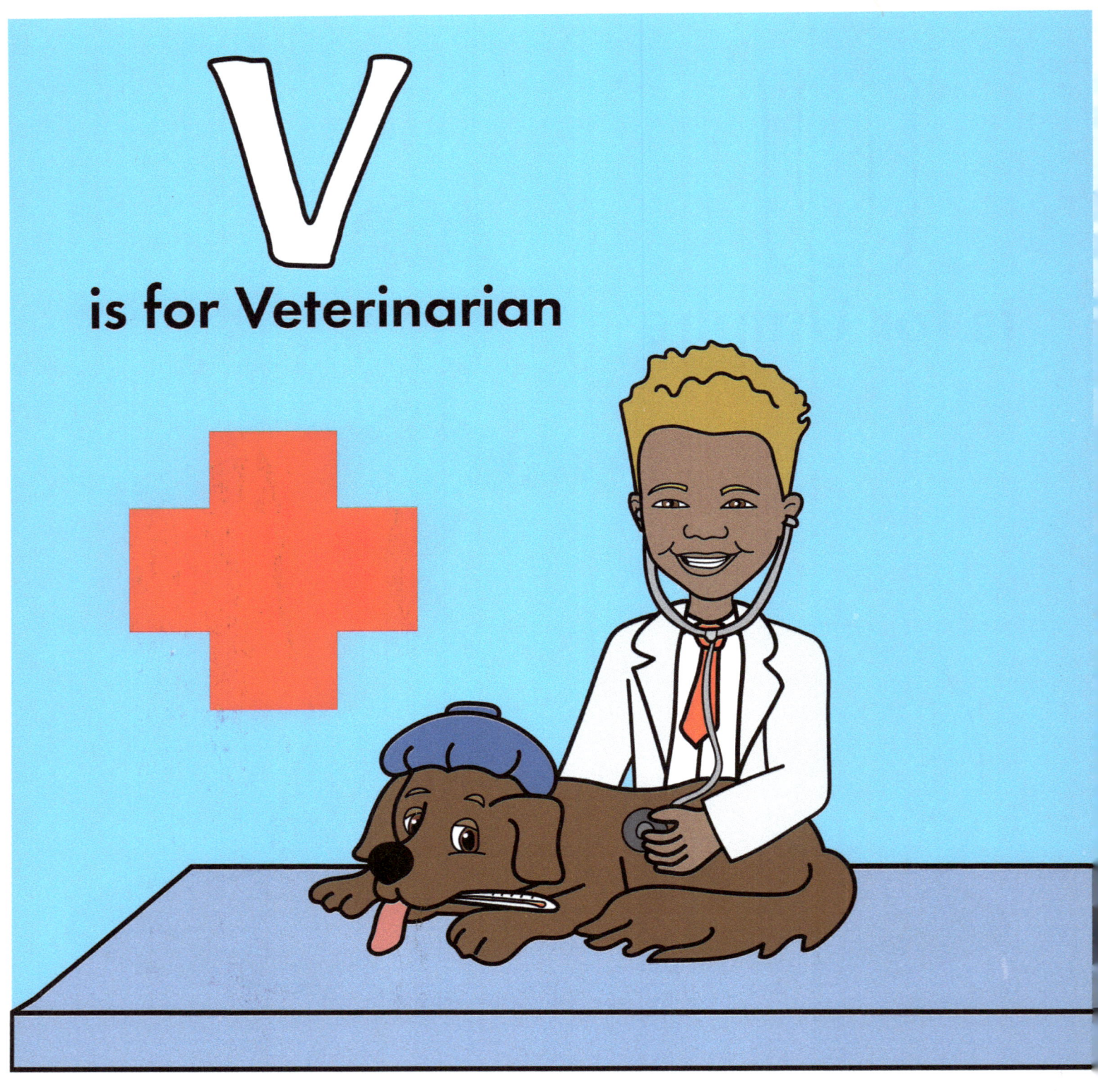

# W
### is for Writer

# X
## is for X-Ray Technician

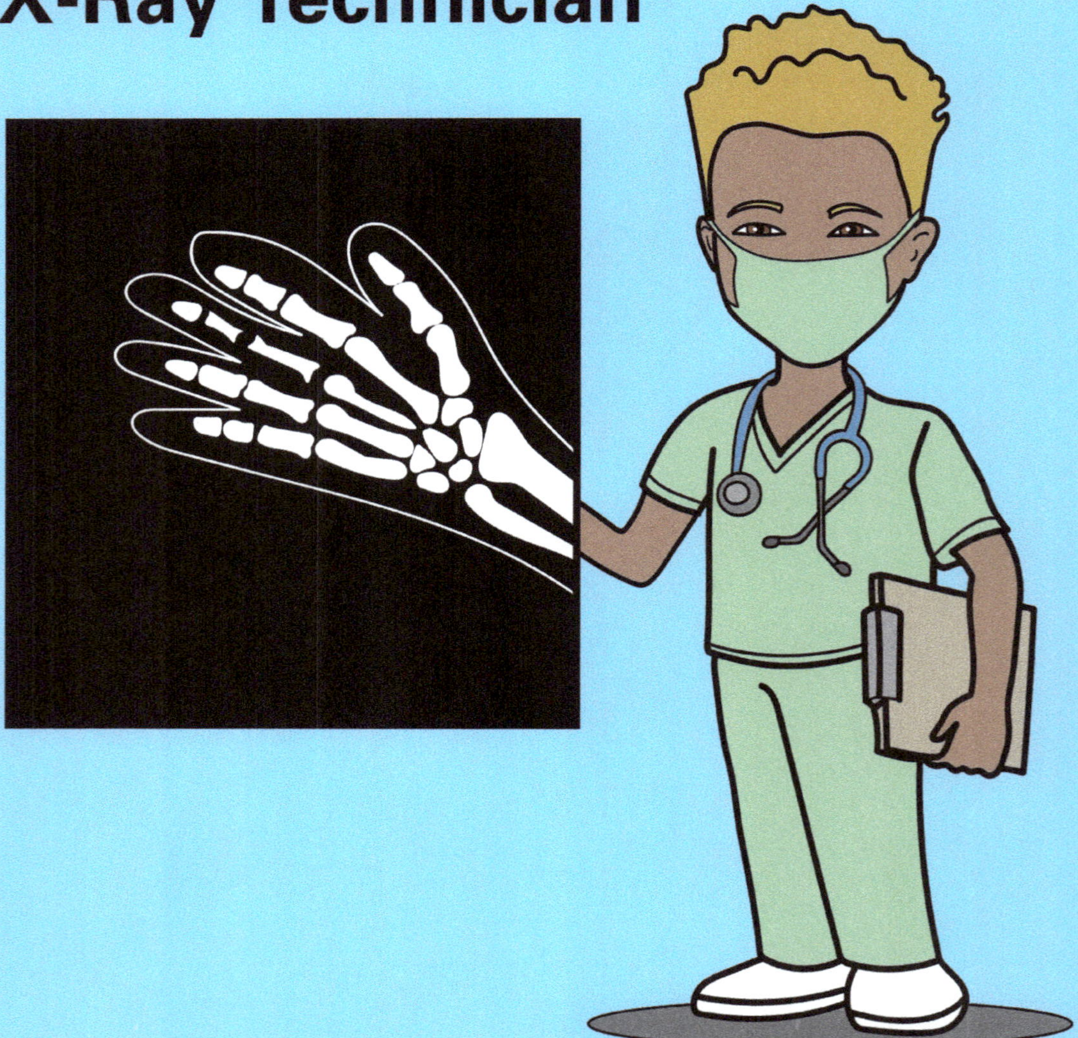

# Y

is for Yachtsman

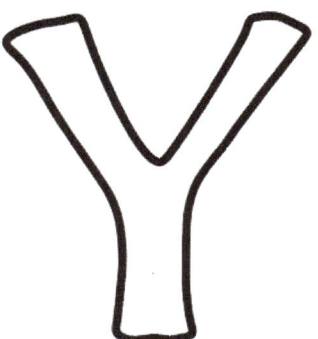

# THE END

www.ingramcontent.com/pod-product-compliance
Lightning Source LLC
Chambersburg PA
CBHW061800290426
44109CB00030B/2912